A
SOCIETY
OF PINES

Published by: Knife Island Publishing, Inc.
                P.O. Box 251277
                Woodbury, MN 55125
                www.KnifeIslandPublishing.com

Author's Note:

A Society of Pines is offered for entertainment purposes only. Any other use of the information contained herein is idiotic and is strictly prohibited.

Printed in the United States of America.

10 9 8 7 6 5 4 3 2 1 First Edition

ISBN 0-9729215-0-8

A
SOCIETY
OF PINES

PHOTOGRAPHED
AND WRITTEN BY
ROBERT SHUTES

To all pines and their friends.

To my family.

And to Lydia,
who inspired me to write.

CONTENTS

ACKNOWLEDGMENTS

Many thanks to everyone who helped make working on A *Society of Pines* such a pleasant experience and very little like work at all. To Bruce Halvorson and the guys at First Photo who helped me catch an eagle. To the crew at the Nemadji Golf Course for trying to make an honest tree out of their Lobster. And to the Highway Patrolmen who were kind enough not to arrest me for standing around on the expressway taking pictures.

To Rick Kollath for his expertise and to Sparky Stensaas for his advice. To Connie Wirta for her encouragement and to Catherine Long my editor who re-introduced me to punctuation marks like commas and semi-colons and tried to help me overcome my tendency to write run on sentences which we worked on for quite a while and finally overcame although it wasn't easy to do at first but it did get easier as time went on and on and I eventually mastered it. To Stan Hooper for his help and many good suggestions.

I am also deeply indebted to Nicholas Mirov and Jean Hasbrouck. Their wonderfully informative book, *The Story of Pines*, provided much of the information that became the Pineology found in A *Society of Pines*.

And this our life, exempt from public haunt,
Finds tongues in trees, books in the running brooks,
Sermons in stones, and good in everything.

William Shakespeare

INTRODUCTION

A Ballerina Pine named Lydia introduced me to the Society of Pines. The first time I saw her she was standing beside the road wearing a green tutu in the golden light of an autumn day. I had been driving by without noticing her for nearly 15 years, and then one day she just stepped out and introduced herself. I chuckled at the thought of a Dancing Pine in a glowing green tutu, and in no time at all we became friends. Then she introduced me to an entire Society of Pines as interesting and as distinctive as she.

Pines are very much intrigued by the Society of People. This is in spite of our history of cutting them down by the millions at Christmas and the annual Pinewood Derby, which they view as positively ghoulish even if it is done by innocent-looking little Cub Scouts. Pines have been trying to understand us ever since the Pilgrims landed at Plymouth Rock, but we have remained ignorant of the ways of the forest until now.

A Society of Pines is presented to the reader with the sincere desire that it will clear up many common misconceptions between the Societies of Pines and People, and help provide a cure for IDD (imagination deficit disorder). It is the author's hope that every pine might call you friend, and greet you with the ancient Pine Blessing:

> *"Yours be the sun and yours be the rain!*
> *Let morning's sweet dew rest upon you.*
> *May your sap e're run strong*
> *After winter's last song,*
> *And seedlings take root all around you."*

pinehood *n* **1.** that state of being which is enjoyed by pines of all types.

Author's Note:
Most trees achieve pinehood by virtue of their birth parents, but this is not always the case. Adoption is not uncommon in Pine Society. Any evergreen, regardless of parentage, that sings the Song of Pines is also regarded as a true pine.

PINEOLOGY –
BASICS

Pines, as all pines know quite well, are the largest and most important family of trees that bear cones. There are about 100 clans in the genus "pinus" of the pine family "pinaceae," and every single member of the family is an evergreen.

Soft pines are also called white pines, or "haploxylon," while the hard pines are known as yellow pines, or "diploxylon." This is absolute nonsense to the pines themselves, who know full well that they are green and don't speak Latin in any case.

LYDIA

Of all the Fine Arts Pines none are more beloved or well known than Lydia the Ballerina Pine. She has taken up a hillside residence at the western end of Lake Superior and is an inspiration to all who know her. It is so easy to admire her indomitable spirit and love of life. Little wonder that she is considered the Grand Dame of all the Dancing Pines. The winds and years may have stripped most of her branches, but a long time ago Lydia decided to don her tutu and dance at the side of the road, in spite of the hard times, in celebration of everything good and beautiful.

When she is moved to dance by the winds blowing off Lake Superior, the way she flounces her tutu is a sight to behold. While some researchers may dispute whether or not pines are able to dance at all, Lydia's legendary grace has settled the issue forever. Lovers of the arts thrill to see the way she sways and floats on the winds of her hillside home.

> *But, oh, she dances such a way!*
> *No sun… is half so fine a sight.*
> *Sir John Suckling*

PINEOLOGY —
SONG OF PINES

A fine and wonderful thing is a pine! The fervent *esprit de cone* that characterizes Pine Society is ingrained into their young at sprouting and is summed up nicely by the Pine Anthem. Called "The Song of Pines," it is whispered with great feeling at every sunrise and sunset.

> *"We are the trees of the forest!*
> *The sky, wind and snows are here for us.*
> *The sun and the rain, and morning's sweet dew.*
> *We are the trees evergreen!"*

Pine Folk think trees with leaves only in summer are just big flowers. Some pines do enjoy having a backdrop of brightly colored leaves in autumn, but most enjoy it even more when those leaves finally fall. This is not so surprising when you consider how much these "flowers" block the pines' view of things and generally get in the way all summer.

It is noteworthy that pines do seem to have a special fondness for birches and poplars. This feature of Pine Society has been commented upon by other researchers and is discussed in this text as well. (See Birch Pines)

And wind, that grand old Harper,
Smote his thunder-harp of pines.

Alexander Smith

THE LEGEND OF
THE PITCH PINE

According to legend, there was a time when pines did not know how to play the woodwind music they are so famous for today. It is said that when the wind came to play in the treetops, nothing came out but noise. Studies confirm that pine trees are somewhat tone deaf, so it is not surprising there was little harmony in the music of early Pine Society. Recent discoveries from the fossil record and accounts from ancient civilizations confirm that what was heard then was not at all like what we hear now when the wind blows through the forest.

A long debate has asked why the harmony of the trees in the wind is so pleasing today, and how it is, that no matter where you are in the forest, the song is the same. Years of careful observation have finally led us to understand this is due to the work of the Pitch Pines. They were the first of the trees to learn how to cup their branches together to sing with the wind, and it was they who taught the other trees to sing together in harmony. They are sometimes called Choir Director or Tuning Fork Pines, and even today the forest is unable to hold a tune without them. They are much loved by other trees and are greatly admired for their perfect pitch.

The development of music was a dramatic advance, and one that has given Pine Society much of its current distinctiveness. Although we now have some understanding of how the Pitch Pines brought harmony to the forest, it remains a mystery how they themselves learned to resonate so beautifully to the earth and the wind. When asked about it, they just smile and whisper a chorus by one of their favorite minstrels (whose roots are entwined with theirs) entitled "Blowing in the Wind."

I cannot see what flowers are at my feet,
Nor what soft incense hangs upon the boughs.

John Keats

PINEOLOGY - FRAGRANCE

No one knows why pines smell so good, but people and pines are both pretty happy about it. The fragrance of a pine forest comes from a class of chemicals called terpenes, from which we get turpentine. Not all pines smell like Pin-Sol though: the Digger Pines of the Sierra Nevada mountains smell like vanilla, the Pinyon Pines of the Southwest smell like zinfandel grapes, and the Rocky Mountain Ponderosa smells like butterscotch. True friends of Pine Society refrain from eating these trees, no matter how good they smell.

In hot weather the volatile essential oils of a pine are released in large quantities. When conditions are just right, this can cause a blue haze to form and linger over the forest. Sometimes people love to linger in a pine forest too. The great German author Goethe felt the fragrance of the pinewoods was a "sweet peace," bestowed from above simply to soothe and comfort mankind. Spend a day in the pines and you'll agree.

JOCK PINES

Jock Pines (no relation to Jack) are the most athletically-inclined members of Pine Society. They are highly disciplined and can be seen waving their branches vigorously for hours at a time to develop the broad "shoulders" they so admire. Other pines simply shrug their own shoulders at this unusual behavior and consider it harmless. It does, after all, help keep these individuals out of cheap taverns and smoky pool halls. This ready acceptance of Jock Pine eccentricity is very much in keeping with Pine Society's high regard for individuality.

There are some instances, however, in which Jock Pines are in conflict with established standards of pine behavior. When Jocks start pumping pitch and pine cones during hot weather, the odor can be overpowering. This doesn't seem to bother the Jock pines much, but the effects on other trees can range from mild wilting of the branches to outright fainting, gagging, and even the loss of greenery. A recent trend in Pine Society has been the development of workout areas for Jock Pines. While this has resulted in some social isolation for the Jock Pines themselves, it is widely hailed as a good solution by everyone else.

POM POM PINES

Pine Tree Society's embrace of modern culture and professional sports has given rise to an entirely new family of pines known as Pom Pom Pines. These can be seen near stadiums where they shake and wave their pom poms enthusiastically to the delight of fans, who seem to thoroughly enjoy the beauty of pine poms. It is unknown whether their vigorous shaking displays have any actual impact on the outcome of stadium games, but they definitely add spectacle value to the event. No one seriously suggests removing them from areas around arenas, and it is a safe bet that the Pom Pom Pines are here to stay.

Because of you we will be glad…
And meet the great adventure with a song.
And you will speed us onward with a cheer
Maurice Baring

GOLF COURSE PINES

Few trees are more shameless or endearing than Golf Course Pines. They are prone to wild exaggerations, but this is usually harmless and can even be entertaining (and quite understandable when you consider the company they keep). The Lobster Pine shown here is trying with all its might to convince everyone at the Nemadji Golf Course that it is a lobster! Since lobsters don't live inland you can be sure it is, at best, a crayfish… but that's how it is with Golf Course Pines. They just can't keep themselves from stretching the truth whenever there is even the slightest chance they might get away with it.

Golf Course Pines do love to tell stories and can be deeply hurt if you don't believe them. When questioned about the accuracy of their accounts, they will often mumble something about "winter rules" and can become quite agitated with those who insist on the factual accuracy of golf course stories. It is usually best to just nod your head and feign belief, unless there is money or honor at stake. Although some claim to have seen Golf Course Pines imitating golfers keeping honest scorecards, this has never been verified. Authorities doubt that Golf Course Pines have any idea at all of what this would even look like.

HIGHWAY PINES

According to the archives of the Pine Historical Society, pine entertainment has changed dramatically in the last one hundred years. This has been due to the advent of the automobile, which most pines find to be endlessly fascinating. Highway Pines love to watch the cars race around and play tag. Many pines do all they can to get front row seats, especially near curves in the road where highway tag is thought to be most exciting. They are especially thrilled when one of the brightly lit "screaming howlers" actually catches one of the plainer cars. Admittedly there is quite a bit of confusion among the pines themselves over what exactly is going on at these times, but that is hardly

surprising. Some pines dispute the notion of "tag" and insist it is really a game of "hide and seek", since the screaming howlers like to hide from the other cars just before chasing them. Many Highway Pines believe that the little yellow coupons given out by the screaming howlers are highly prized driving awards and that the flashing lights represent a singular honor. Another opinion is that the howlers are delivering some very bad news to the drivers (perhaps something about the stock market). This view is rejected as implausible and cynical by most pines, who at last report, still have a lot of confidence in the market.

What's in a name? That which we call a rose
By any other name would smell as sweet.

William Shakespeare

Author's Note:
This is a nice thought, but pines don't read
Shakespeare, so you should be careful to address
them properly.

PINEOLOGY – NAMES

Proper names must be used when greeting or striking up conversations with Pine Folk. Using names that are incorrect or offensive to the pines themselves is a sure conversation stopper and has caused much needless hurt and misunderstanding. Latin and botanical names should be avoided since these are social affectations rejected by virtually all pines, except for those pretentious types that are widely (and correctly) regarded by other pines as social climbers and snobs. Rest assured that this text uses only those names that are favored by pines and to which they will gladly respond.

Author's Note:
Once you have established a cordial relationship with pines you should avoid needling or making pun of them unless you are very sure of your friendship.

NO WAY PINES

Casual observers have often been heard to exclaim, "There's no way that's a pine tree!" the first time they encounter one of the wild and Woolly Mammoth Pines that inhabit North America. This classic "No way!" response gave rise to their common name, the No Way Pine. In Pine Society, however, it is well known that they themselves prefer to be called Woolly Mammoths.

No Way Pines exhibit significant departures from common notions of pineness. Emphatic individuality is a trait admired in many pine families, and those who adopt unique branch profiles without regard to fashion trends seem to relish their "cussedly independent" reputation. Those who embrace this branch set declare that it makes for a comfortable, albeit unconventional, life. In their view, no self-respecting pine should waste time or effort trying to grow its branches into the "right" look. Suggest otherwise to a No Way Pine and your chance of making a friend is nil. Applaud their creativity, and you will be honored as a true Friend of Pines.

BIG BRANCH PINES

Big Branch Pines are friends of eagles. In youth and mid-life they are content to grow and display their branches on hillsides and in open places where they can best be viewed against a sweeping expanse of sky. It is clear that they thoroughly enjoy the admiration of trees and people alike, and branch display is their primary activity for many decades. We now understand that when they reach late adulthood, these wonderful giants begin to prefer companionship to admiration, and at this point they undergo a striking social transformation: elder Big Branch Pines enjoy the visits of eagles.

Having experienced the pleasant company of eagles, many Big Branch Pines begin grooming themselves to be attractive perches for the great birds and throw off needles and branches willy-nilly to that end. This is done in the hope of attracting eagle visits, and is especially the case with those trees that have grown old on barren hillsides and fields, far from the company of other trees. Pineologists are divided on the question of whether this Big Branch affinity for eagles is because they like having their branches scratched or simply enjoy the company. What is known is that the arrangement seems to work quite well for both parties, who are often seen spending entire afternoons together, chatting about things that matter to eagles and great trees.

Silver and gold are not the only coin;
virtue too passes current all over the world.

Euripides

PINEOLOGY - MONEY

Pines don't have much use for money and rarely, if ever, carry cash. But there was a coin minted in Massachusetts in the 1600s that was named after them. The Pine Tree Shilling was minted between the execution of one English king in 1649 and the coronation of another in 1660. Since it was illegal for anyone but a king to mint coins, the colonists were careful to stamp the coins with the date 1652. This let them claim they really weren't breaking any laws because there wasn't a king on the throne then. That proved to be a good way for the colonists to stay alive, and pines of that era were pretty happy about the whole affair, since they were nicely engraved on every coin that was minted.

WITNESS PINES

Few trees are more utterly dependable than a Witness Pine. Because of their integrity and reliability, Witness Pines have provided invaluable assistance to the Society of People throughout history. The Witness Pine shown here has been leading the way to a survey marker since the 1800s. When Wisconsin was still a territory and was being surveyed prior to statehood, the survey crew could not place the section marker in a bog, so they wrote down its precise location in relation to the Witness Pine pictured. This tree has been carrying out its duty faithfully ever since and has not left its post even once.

Author's Note:

This Witness Pine, and the Honking Pine shown elsewhere are both mature and beautiful trees with one thing in common: Both were scheduled to be cut down by highway crews widening roads, and both were saved from that fate by highway engineers who appreciated the value of a good tree and insisted that they be allowed to remain standing.

> Woodman, spare that tree!
> Touch not a single bough!
> In youth it sheltered me,
> And I'll protect it now.
>
> **George Pope Morris**

BEGGING PINES

Pine folk are generally a pretty self-reliant bunch. Most pines go about the business of sprouting branches, needles, and cones with no outside help at all. It is rare to find one that needs or wants much help with grooming, raising their young, or anything else that pines busy themselves with. This gritty independence is one of the finest characteristics of pine society and helps account for its resilience and survival in the most rugged environments. Many of the most well-known pine ballads celebrate this very quality and help perpetuate what is regarded as one of the highest of pine virtues.

Now and then, though, one may encounter a pine that has fallen upon such hard times that it feels compelled to resort to panhandling. Known as Hard Times, Panhandling, or Begging Pines, they can be identified by one large branch held out palm up in hopes of getting a little help from passing motorists or even from another tree. Begging is usually fruitless, since most motorists fail to notice them, and other pines have little to give. Many students of Pine Society feel that the Begging Pines continue this non-productive behavior anyway just to help pass the time. They are generally considered to be harmless, but if you do observe a Begging Pine in your neighborhood, most authorities recommend locking your doors as a reasonable precaution against theft.

HITCHING PINES

Hitch-Hiking Pines are members of the Hard Times Pines family and are closely related to the Begging Pines. The Hitch-Hiker shown here was observed trying to get a ride on the freeway just south of a major casino, where it was rumored to have lost everything at the Blackjack tables. This Hitch-Hiker was in no mood to either confirm or deny the rumor while casino officials declared that having to hitch a ride was a small price to pay for the all the entertainment provided.

Field identification of the Hitch-Hiking Pine is not difficult. One need only search the highways near casinos to find pines with one branch held out in typical hitch-hiker fashion. This is risky behavior for these pines, since the only motorists known to stop are loggers whose motives are clear. Since escape in these situations is nearly impossible, Pine Society encourages its members to be responsible in casinos. And win or lose, to avoid hitch-hiking altogether.

Waste not, want not, is a maxim I would teach.
Let your watchword be dispatch,
and practice what you preach.
Do not let your chances like sunbeams pass you by,
for you never miss the water till the well runs dry.

Rowland Howard

PINEOLOGY - WATER

Pines have learned to be pretty careful with their resources, especially water. They need to exhale water in order to live, but they also need to keep plenty of water on board. The system they use to breathe in and out and still preserve their water supply is a model of simplicity and wisdom.

Every pine needle has little shutters (botanists call them "stomata," but this is only because botanists tend to have a hard time with English). When pines wake up in the morning, the first thing they do is open their shutters and go to work making sugars from water, light and air. Then they close their shutters again at the end of the day and settle in for a good night's sleep.

Pines breathe out so much water when they work in hot weather that it would be fatal if they didn't have enough sense to know when to quit. The water cost of working in hot weather is so high that most pines close up shop early and lock their shutters long before they are in danger of dehydrating. Then they hold their breath for the rest of the day! This sounds like it would be hard to do, but pines are so good at it that they make it look easy.

LAKESIDE PINES

Lakeside Pines love peaceful mornings and the stillness of calm evenings. They also appreciate sun-splashed waters as a backdrop for their own greenery (not to mention the convenience of having a mirror-smooth surface handy for grooming). The view is great, and the air is sweet near the water; a combination that is an irresistible draw for many pines. Happily settled into their lakeside homes, it is clear these individuals enjoy their life beside still waters.

On the other hand, there is a growing awareness among pineologists that Lakeside Pines are also thrill seekers! This is especially the case with the Great Lakes Pines. The serene North Shore Pine shown here is the very same North Shore Pine that can be heard shrieking with delight and flailing its branches in near hysteria when the Northeast winds begin to howl in off Lake Superior! Many of these pines barely cling to the rocks by their toenails, but like to keep their branches up in the air during the wildest of the so-called "roller coaster storms," and don't even try to hold on with their branches! While this may seem to be out of character for trees known to be so careful with their own survival, the exhilaration these pines experience no doubt contributes to their vitality and *joie de vivre.*

A lake, the blue-eyed Walden,
That doth smile most tenderly upon its neighbor pines

William Ellery Channing

HERO PINES

Pines admire a fearless leader as much as anyone, and pine lore has more than its share of heroes and captains courageous. Sometimes these are visionary types who long for adventure and far horizons (which is all well and good), but it can be a struggle to get others to come along. The rallying cry of Pine Folk has always been, "Hold your ground! Everyone! Don't move an inch!" Pines especially love leaders who can express this well, since holding their ground is pretty much all they can do anyway.

Every so often there comes a leader, like the Heroic Pine pictured here, who valiantly tries to lead his comrades on a daring adventure. For some time now he has been challenging them to charge up the hill and cross right over the highway! Maybe go all the way to Canada even and visit some distant relatives. So far, though, no one is paying much attention to him. Once he has had time to reconsider things, there is little doubt that he will take up the old rallying cry, and be recognized as a true Hero after all.

Heroism feels and never reasons
and therefore is always right.

Ralph Waldo Emerson

*She swore, in faith, 'twas strange, 'twas passing strange,
'twas pitiful, 'twas wondrous pitiful.*

William Shakespeare

PINEOLOGY – MYTH

The ancient Greeks were so fond of pines that they even made a place for them in their mythology. Pitys was a lovely little wood nymph whose job was tending pine trees. She had a lover named Boreas who was god of the north wind; but she was also fond of Pan, who was a lot of fun and was pretty good on the flute.

One day Pitys and Boreas were having a lovers' quarrel when the subject of Pan came up. Boreas, a cold and blustery fellow, lost his temper and threw poor Pitys against a rocky outcrop, where she took root and became a pine tree. To this day the north wind still breaks pine branches in anger, and the drops of resin that flow are the tear drops of Pitys as she weeps over her sad fate and loves lost. Today there is a pine that grows near the Black Sea in Eastern Europe that is named Pinus Pityusa in her memory.

FENCING PINES

While some commentators may have declared that pines are not good fencing material, there is incontrovertible proof to the contrary. The Musketeer Pines are fond of assuming the classic *en garde* stance and taking a stab at it. Although Pine Society is essentially non-violent, most pines love a good adventure story. Swashbuckling heroes are always in style. The D'Artagnan Pine shown here (Captain of the Tree Musketeers) is a favorite with pines and motorists alike. He displays the courage and flair that Fencing Pines are famous for.

Without a sign, his sword the brave man draws.

Alexander Pope

HONKING PINES

Along with Bigfoot, the Loch Ness monster, and UFO sightings, many legends persist about Honking Pines said to inhabit the great northern forests. To date, though, there has not been a single confirmed sighting of a true Honking Pine. This is not surprising considering the pine aversion to loud noises in general and car horns in particular. Pines are in favor of whispering, sighing in the wind and creaking a little on cold mornings, but honking is frowned upon in Pine Society. It is also highly unlikely that any pines have ever developed the technology needed to honk.

What many people have confused with the so-called Honking Pines are in fact Honkee Pines. These trees can occasionally be found standing near major highways, where, for reasons not yet fully understood, they provoke passing motorists to honk at them! These horn blasts can result in chronic anxiety and sleep deprivation for the beleaguered Honkee Pine if motorists are not careful to sound their horns with courtesy and discretion.

The proper way to salute a Honkee Pine is with several light taps on the horn. This should be initiated while the passing vehicle is still several hundred yards away so as not to startle the Honkee. Pines that have been subjected to persistent, sustained horn blasts at close range often develop neurotic behaviors, which have been known to develop into full blown psychotic episodes. This is believed to be a direct result of sleep deprivation. Since pines like to sleep from sunset to sunrise it is best to pass by them silently at those times. If you do happen to notice a Honkee napping at mid-day, common decency dictates that you not disturb it then either.

Author's Note: *The pine pictured here lives on the North Shore of Lake Superior, where it is known and loved by locals and tourists alike.*

MOSQUITO PINES

Unlike the legends about Honking Pines (which have been thoroughly debunked), the stories that persist in the northwoods about Mosquito Pines are horrifyingly true. These frightening tales have been passed on around campfires without number as generations of outdoor enthusiasts warn their children to be ever on guard against these evil giants: "They'll suck you as dry as a shriveled up old leaf!"

All mosquitoes must make at least one pilgrimage in their short lives to receive instruction and inspiration beneath the awful boughs of a giant Mosquito Pine. On warm and moonlit nights, it is sometimes possible to observe hordes of them swarming around a Mosquito Pine in a frenzy of beating wings and bloodthirsty beaks.

While Pine Society claims to be neutral about the Mosquito Pines in its midst, it is undeniable that many stands of pines harbor and provide cover for these dreadful creatures. This issue has caused serious strains between the Society of Pines and the Society of People and will require painstaking and difficult negotiation to resolve, but as long as diplomatic channels are kept open, there is hope for progress.

Sage-brush to kindle with, quaking-asp to glow,
Pine-roots to last until the dawn-winds blow.
Oh smoke full of fancies, and dreams gone to smoke,
At the camp-fires dead long ago.

   Robert Cameron Rogers

THE ONE-SIDED PINE

Of all the trees in the forest, none are more feared than the dreaded One-Sided Pine. These are true predators who will pounce on the unwary without warning and slowly render them unconscious with lengthy and mind-numbing monologues. Although attacks by One-Sided Pines are rarely fatal, the experience can be traumatic. Human survivors can be identified by their dilated pupils, shallow respirations and rapid heart rate. Pines who encounter these Trees of Prey often develop Brown Needle Syndrome and may lose large chunks of bark. Many innocent ten-point bucks have been blamed for scraping the bark from young saplings that were really the victims of One-Sided Pine attacks. Trees and humans alike typically shun social contacts for several weeks following contact with a One-Sided Pine due to fear of another attack. The long-term effects are not known, but while they are not thought to be serious, more research is clearly needed.

Field experts agree the best strategy is to avoid areas One-Sided Pines are known to inhabit. If you are unfortunate enough to encounter a One-Sided Pine on the prowl, you must immediately walk the other way while pretending not to have seen it. Do not try to strike up a conversation! Survivors report that the only escape is to fake a heart attack or seizure and then roll or crawl away while avoiding direct eye contact. Tree-wise individuals know that early detection and avoidance of One-Sided Pines is essential to safety in the woods.

PINEOLOGY -
MARRIAGE

Pines do not marry but manage to have a lot of fun anyway. Marriage as we know it does not exist in pine society because each pine is equipped with both male and female parts. It may seem a bit odd to us, but the system they have worked out is pretty effective for trees, who want to reproduce but have a hard time moving around the forest looking for a mate.

Male cones are found high in the tree's crown and produce golden clouds of pollen that waft through the forest quite nicely on spring breezes. Female cones are larger and woodier than the males, and contain seeds hoping to be fertilized by all that pollen floating around. The union of floating pollen with waiting seeds usually results in a nice crop of new pine sprouts every year. Sorting out parentage, though, is nearly impossible: no one even tries. Needless to say, paternity suits are rare in the Society of Pines; there are, however, legions of lawyers working to develop what they view as a huge potential market.

Once the whole dizzying affair is over, both male and female cones die and fall to the ground, but the trees themselves live on. That's just how it is with pines, and nothing else would make any sense to them at all.

HUGGING PINES

Despite a lot of talk these days about "tree huggers," this only describes behavior between people and trees, since pines themselves rarely engage in hugging. The lack of hugging in Pine Society is not clearly understood since they are quite fond of each other. Some researchers feel it may have something to do with their Scandinavian roots, but this is simply conjecture. What is well known, however, is that most pines do not welcome hugs from people and will grow their branches all the way down to the ground to prevent it.

Hugging is socially awkward for most pines (who consider it a bit sappy at best), which is one reason it is avoided. Nevertheless, many of the larger and older pines (notably the Big Branch and Air Pines) will tolerate these shows of affection from people. But even they are a little embarrassed by it. If you do feel like hugging a pine tree, a much better alternative is to just give it a few good pats on the back of its trunk, like NFL football players do after each play.

PORKY PINES

There is little doubt that the epidemic of obesity in America has been paralleled by a similar trend in Pine Society. Smoking has never been a serious health issue among pines. Those who are foolish enough to "experiment" with it disappear in flames immediately after lighting up. This has been an effective deterrent since no Smoking Pines have survived long enough to offer a drag to their friends. Fast food, on the other hand, is a whole different story.

What could be better than the pleasure of a big juicy bacon double cheeseburger, a large order of french fries and a chocolate malt? Haven't we all caved in from time to time? For pines, whose diet historically has been dirt and water, the temptation is overwhelming. And the presence in their midst of such delicacies has given rise to a whole new species of tree known as the Porky Pine, whose rounded profile is its defining characteristic.

A variety of approaches have been tried to help the Porky Pines slim down, but most have failed. Neither education, counseling, meditation, hypnotism nor even drugs have had any real impact on the dietary habits of these trees. Until an effective treatment is found, there is little that can be done short of uprooting these individuals and replanting them far from the parking lots they love. Whether or not the Porky Pines will acquiesce remains to be seen, and many who follow this issue are convinced it will end up in the high courts.

GUM DROP PINES

The Common House Pine or Domesticated Pine is affectionately called the Gum Drop Pine by those who raise them as pets. Although it is well known that most pines prefer wild places, many now inhabit locales that are dominated by the presence of human civilization. Gum Drop Pines thus endure all manner of grooming and shaping by their "owners" and are far removed from any hint of what is generally regarded as normal in Pine Society. (The only vestige of pinehood they appear to retain is their essential greenness.)

Many pines are appalled by the indignities visited upon Gum Drop Pines and wonder why they tolerate all the pruning that goes with the position. Nevertheless, it does seem that many Domesticated Pines are content with their lot and even learn to enjoy all the pampering and grooming. While they may be disdained by other pines as frivolous dandies, the Gum Drops just shrug their branches in fine pine stoicism and say, "Hey, it's a living." Generally considered to be quite tame, they have been known to turn on their owners, and sprout all manner of wild and haphazard branches if left untended for even short periods of time.

Your children are not your children. They are the sons and daughters of life's longing for itself.

Kahlil Gibran

PINEOLOGY - CHILDREN

Pine children begin life safely nestled in the petals of their mother cone. Once a seed has been fertilized it can take a year or two before it feels ready to float away and start life on its own. This is a once in a lifetime chance for the potential seedling. Those who don't sprout will never sing the Song of Pines, but their hopes mingle with the soil, and their unfulfilled dreams become part of the Song.

Most pines end up growing pretty close to their parents and rarely root more than 100 yards away. This gives the older generation plenty of opportunity to whisper encouragement and advice while preserving the personal space and peace of mind pines are known to cherish.

PUNK PINES

Continuing its trend of steady assimilation into American culture, Pine Society has recently been affected by the punk rock phenomenon. This can be seen in the wild branch "do's" affected by many Punk Pines. The young, who style their upper branches in outlandish shapes (to the consternation of the older generation), never fail to point out that this isn't so very different than what their parents themselves were doing just one generation ago. That makes it a bit hard for the older trees to say too much.

Mature pines have discovered that it's risky business to sprout a lot of branches way up high, since one good storm is often enough to blow the whole business right off. Having learned this through painful experience older pines generally avoid keeping much branch at treetop height. While some pines do get agitated by youthful outbursts of foolish branching, most are content to let the young Punk Pines have their fun. Adult pines know that the years are full of lessons, which the winds never fail to bestow.

It is the lofty pine that by the storm is oftener tossed;
Towers fall with heavier crash which higher soar.

Horace

SHOUTING PINES

Shouting Pines are closely related to the dreaded One-Sided Pines discussed elsewhere in this text. They are the loudest of the pines, and communicate by shouting rather than whispering or sighing, which are the accepted norms of behavior in Pine Society. Their outlandish conduct tends to drive other pines away, which then causes the Shouting or Loudmouth Pines to increase their volume levels even more. Some researchers believe the Shouting Pines have actually damaged their own hearing by all the noise they make. Whether or not this is true, the fact remains that Loudmouth Pines don't listen well.

Shouting Pines were relatively rare until the last half of the twentieth century. At that time, the popularity of youth athletics resulted in a dramatic rise in the number of Screaming and Shouting Parent Pines, who then passed on this unfortunate trait to their seedlings. Thankfully, a grassroots movement has quietly been holding meetings in an attempt to reverse this unhappy trend and encourage a return to whispering and sighing softly in the wind.

Avoid loud and aggressive persons, they are vexations to the spirit.

Desiderata, by Max Ehrmann

Ein Fichtenbaum Steht Einsam

A pine tree stands so lonely
In the North where the high winds blow,
He sleeps; and the whitest blanket
Wraps him in ice and snow,

Heinrich Heine

PINEOLOGY - WINTER

Winter is a time of reflection in Pine Society. There is little point in trying to work when the snows come, the days are short and the sun is pale. From winter solstice to spring equinox, pines like to bask in the snow and not do much of anything at all, except enjoy the goodness of Pinehood. But, they are not asleep as some have wrongly supposed. While it is true that the Pine Anthem is not sung aloud in winter, it continues to be deeply felt and is still in the thoughts of Pine Society at every sunrise and sunset.

Pine thoughts in the season of snows are known only to pines and have never been shared with human researchers. Evergreens know that some things are beyond words and can only truly be felt anyway. A favorite Pine Saying that is often heard sums it up this way, "In summer guard your water, and in winter guard your thoughts."

CHRISTMAS TREES

The importance of Christmas Trees to people has been a source of both pride and anxiety in Pine Society. Christmas is called the "Bonfire of the Virgins" season among pines, whose understanding of the annual sap letting is limited. They do know that something in the Society of People demands a yearly appeasement and suspect it has something to do with the large number of people who gather at shopping malls to celebrate. Although it is thought to be a great honor to be a Christmas Tree, most pines are quite relieved when they reach the age at which their youth and virginity are past, and they are no longer eligible. While it is nice to be young and beautifully shaped, it is even better to be ignored during the Time of Cutting.

Pine Society holds that the days of a Christmas Tree are filled with celebrations and luxury far beyond anything other pines ever experience. Thankfully, few Christmas Pines discover that the presents stacked beneath their branches are not for them until their final moments. Pines that know what happens next are careful not to broadcast their views for fear of being labeled irreverent and crazy.

BIRCH PINES

Birch Pines are so called because of their well-known affinity for birch trees. What is little known are their reasons. A recently published study in National Pineographic suggests that vanity lies at the root of the relationship between pines and white birches. In it the author asserts that pines enjoy the presence of these trees because white birch bark provides such a pleasing fashion accent to the dark green of the pines. Interviews with birches indicate that they enjoy the proximity of pines for exactly the same reason!

Some critics contend that issues of vanity and style are too frivolous to account for the "proximity" phenomenon, but at this point, it is clear that the vanity theory explains the pine fondness for birches better than any other model yet presented. This new-found understanding also explains the more subdued relationship that pines have with poplars, who are known as "lesser birches" in the Society of Pines.

Ah, happy world, where all things live
Creatures of one great law, indeed;
Bound by strong roots…

Harriet Prescott Spofford

PINEOLOGY - ROOTS

Nearly all of a pine tree is visible to the eye; no artifice here at all. Only 10% of a pine is below ground as root system. Lots of roots right on the surface and a central tap root to anchor it and drink deep. It is said that pines figured out this system early in their history and see no reason to change now.

While most of a pine's root system is on the surface, its roots intermingle with the roots of its neighbors to form an underground network that ties them all together. When the winds are strong, pine trees have agreed to stand or fall together knowing it's a good way to stay alive in stormy times.

And if I should live to be
The last leaf upon the tree
In the spring,
Let them smile as I do now,
At the old forsaken bough
Where I cling.
Oliver Wendell Holmes

PINEOLOGY — LONGEVITY

Some pines die young. Some live a long, long time. Old age for a Bristlecone Pine is somewhere between 4000–5000 years, while Monterey Pines live for about 100 years, if they're lucky. In old age, pines begin to dry up and have more trouble breathing. As they get older they are more prone to diseases, and sometimes they just get weak and die from old age.

The oldest living things in the world are Bristlecone Pines. Long before any of us ever saw the light of day these old pines were alive to skies and sunsets we can only imagine. Before Rome or even the Pyramids were built, the Bristlecone pines were securing themselves to high rocky places in the American Southwest. They are still there today. Remarkably tenacious these old pines.

> *Let me grow lovely growing old-*
> *So many fine things do:*
> *Laces, and ivory, and gold,*
> *and silks need not be new.*
>
> Karle Wilson Baker

GRANDMA PINES

No one sets a better table than a Grandma Pine. Their cooking is legendary, and they are known for their love of getting everyone together. In every season, pines can be observed gathering at Grandma's, in groups large and small, to share old memories and make new ones. It's little wonder so many like to get together at her place.

While many commentators have noted the sighing and whispering in the wind that pines are famous for, Grandma's Pines frequently can be heard to erupt in loud and uproarious laughter. It is believed by most Pineologists that this departure from typical pine behavior is actually beneficial, and should be encouraged to promote healthy cones and longevity. Grandma's Pines themselves have always known it's a good thing to be rooted in laughter and in the company of friends and family.

A GLOSSARY OF PINE

alpine *n* 1. a plant native to alpine or boreal regions 2. Albert Pine (abbreviation); near relative to Jack

compine *v* 1. to mix or place two evergreens together

concupine *n* 1. female consort pine, often young and shapely

cones *n* 1. reproductive organs of pines that produce seeds and pollen

conedom *n* 1. the entire family of cones 2. unreliable method of seedling control

conespiracy theory *n* 1. bizarre belief system, sometimes true (see pine nut)

conical *adj* 1. cone shaped 2. Humorous or funny to pines

conifer *n* 1. evergreen trees with cones and needles

coniferophyte *n* 1. a coniferous plant, or God forbid, its remains

conification *n* 1. act or process of becoming cone shaped 2. to get coned (really)

curvature of the pine *n* 1. orthopedic condition common in Lumbago Pines

evergreen *adj* 1. pine characteristic of greenness at all times

ex-cone *n* 1. pine with a past 2. seedling with criminal record

falling down trunk *n* **1.** pine unable to stand upright due to intoxication

forest *n* **1.** entire community of pines, the pinnacle of pine civilization (see Gump)

Friend of Pines *n* **1.** term of endearment for allies of Pine Society

green card *n* **1.** residency card that allows Friends of Pines to stay in forest

Gump, Forest *n* **1.** most renowned forest of modern times, "Run Forest, run!"

knotty pine *n* **1.** decorative paneling, prized for attractive appearance **2.** pine that exhibits childish or unruly behavior

legal limb it *n* **1.** amount of foliage that may be legally removed from a pine

legally trunk *n* **1.** pine devoid of branches **2.** any pine that exceeds legal "limb it"

limb it *v* **1.** to remove the branches and needles of a pine

nose cone *n* **1.** re-entry vehicle used by early astronauts **2.** nasal piercing seen on aboriginal and punk pines

opine *v* **1.** to express an opinion **2.** poetic expression of pine affection

pinal exam *n* **1.** test required of all seedlings prior to achieving pinehood

pine *n* **1.** any tree of the genus Pinus of the family Pinaceae **2.** any evergreen heard singing the "Song of Pines"

pine *v* **1.** to lose health or vigor, to "pine away **2.** to yearn for the unattainable

pineal gland *n* **1.** cone shaped endocrine gland attached to the brain, believed to enable mammals to think like pines. In reptiles is similar in structure to an eye.

pine bark *n* **1.** the bark of a pine covering its trunk and branches **2.** abnormal vocalizations rarely heard in Pine Society

pine barrens *n* **1.** area wooded with pines **2.** *slang* for "pine barings", nudist pines

pine coffee *n* **1.** pines are not known to drink coffee **2.** *slang* for "pie and coffee"

pine colada *n* **1.** mixed drink popular with vacationing pines *jts*

pine comb *n* **1.** grooming aid used by pines to style branches *jts*

pine cone *n* **1.** the cone of a pine tree

pine cone fish *n* **1.** small sluggish fish of the Monocentris family, found near Japan

pinedrop *n* **1.** leafless wintergreen plant with drooping white flowers. Pine Society denies any kinship to pinedrops **2.** quasi-military operation in which pine seedlings are airlifted into remote areas where they are needed.

pine grosbeak *n* **1.** a large grosbeak *Pinicola enucleator* that lives in coniferous forests

pine grouse *n* **1.** the dusky grouse **2.** complaining pine

pinehood *n* **1.** that state of being which is enjoyed by pines of all types.

pineland *n* **1.** area dominated by pines, called homeland by patriotic pines

pine marten *n* **1.** slender-bodied carnivore that hunts in trees

pine mast *n* **1.** synonym for pine cones **2.** any large gathering of pines

pinene *n* **1.** aromatic hydrocarbon in turpentine

pine needle *n* **1.** pine greenery, looks sharp when used for styling purposes **2.** the "leaf" of a pine that carries out work of photosynthesis

pine nut *n* **1.** edible seed of pinyon or other pines **2.** pine given to odd or extreme views

pineology *n* **1.** scientific study of the personality and social life of pines

pinery *n* **1.** pine forest or grove **2.** fashionable arrangements of pine branches

pinesap *n* **1.** parasitic herbs of the wintergreen family (see pinedrops) **2.** term of derision for socially inept pines

pine siskin *n* **1.** North American finch (Carduelis pinus) that lives among pines

pine snake *n* **1.** black and white constricting snake found among pines on the East Coast **2.** pine villains, widely despised e.g. lawyers, stockbrokers, used cone salesmen, etc.

pin-sol *n* **1.** liquid essence of pine "eau de pine", pine perfume **2.** used by other species as cleaning solution

pine straw *n* 1. dried pine needles 2. opening move of gunslinger pines

pine tar *n* 1. tar obtained from destructive distillation of pine wood 2. fate regarded as capital punishment in Pine Society 3. common pine insult "a pail of pine tar"

pinetentiary *n* 1. place where bad pines go (see ex-cone)

pine the sky *n* 1. *slang* for "pie in the sky", (see pine snakes, esp. stockbroker)

Pine Tree Flag *n* 1. flag of Massachussetts, flown on ships in Revolutionary times

Pine Tree State *n* 1. nickname for Maine 2. pinehood, a state of perfection

pinetum *n* 1. a plantation of pines maintained for scientific purposes 2. rallying cry of Porky Pines, often heard near dumpsters

pine wool *n* 1. fiber obtained by steaming pine needles

pinex *n* 1. cough syrup made with pine tar, very good mixed with brandy

piney woods *n* 1. pinelands with a southern accent

pine r square *n* 1. *slang* for mathematical formula πr^2

punch trunk *v* 1. confusion often seen in pugilistic pines 2. striking pine with fist

red pine *n* 1. North American Pine (Pinus resinosa) 2. any pine with tendency to lean to the left

repine *v* 1. to feel dispirited or melancholy 2. to long for something

root *v* 1. to cheer 2. to send down roots 3. "to take root"

(see root seller)

root seller *n* 1. unsavory character 2. merchant of pine roots 3. ghoul (see pine snake)

scone *n* 1. English pastry 2. *slang* for "it's a cone"

scotch pine *n* 1. pine with drinking problem

scrap *n* 1. pine insult, term of derision 2. scatological *slang* for " it's_____"

seedling *n* 1. newly sprouted pine 2. new ex-cone

seedy *adj* 1. having many seeds

seedy character *n* 1. pine compliment

sno-cone *n* 1. flavored ice confection found at carnivals, state fairs, etc. 2. *slang* for "is no cone", as in "she's nice but she sno-cone."

spine *n* 1. *slang* for "it's a pine" 2. *slang* for espionage "sneaking and spying"

spineless *adj* 1. *slang* for "it's pineless"; designates area devoid of pines 2. cowardly

splinter group *n* 1. notorious pines, known for getting under people's skin

spruced up *adj* 1. obsessively symmetrical branch displays suitable for spruces but less commonly seen in pines

supine *adj* 1. lying on the back facing upward 2. Susan Pine (abbreviation), sister to Alpine 3. pine involved in frequent lawsuits

trunk *n* 1. main stem of a pine 2. intoxicated pine

white pine *n* 1. tall growing North American Pine (Pinus strobes) 2. pine with limited ability to jump

SUBMISSIONS

To nominate a favorite pine for inclusion in future editions of
A Society of Pines, please complete and return this form.

Name of Pine (if known):

_____

Location of Pine:

_____

_____

Personal Profile of Pine: (include accomplishments,
talents, unique characteristics, etc)

_____

_____

_____

_____

_____

Photographs:

Please include a color photograph of nominated pine.
All Pines nominated will be considered for inclusion in
subsequent editions of *A Society of Pines* but submissions
without photographs are at a distinct disadvantage. The
author and editorial committee will attempt to return
photos if you include a self-addressed/stamped return
envelope. Do not be surprised if you never get the
picture back if we really like it.

Sponsor Information: Nomination forms should include
sponsor's name, address and telephone. Please include
e-mail address if you have one.

Mail to: Knife Island Publishing
P.O. Box 251277
Woodbury, MN 55125

Online Submissions: bob@knifeislandpublishing.com

AFTER DINNER DULL?

Looking for something out of the ordinary for your meeting or after dinner speech? The slide show that illustrates the characters and creation of *A Society of Pines* makes for an enjoyable and unforgettable evening. The author is also an experienced public speaker who presents his material with wry humor and warmth. Your group will never forget their evening with Pine Society and will talk about it for years to come.

For more information or to reserve a date for your meeting or group, contact the author on-line at: bob@knifeislandpublishing.com.

ORDER FORM

To order additional copies of *A Society of Pines,* or to send one as a gift, order online (www.KnifeislandPublishing.com) or complete and mail this form to:

Knife Island Publishing, Inc.
P.O. Box 251277
Woodbury, MN 55125

Number of copies _____ ($17.95/copy plus $3.95 S/H)

Ship to: _____

_____

_____

Bill to: _____

_____

_____

Payment: CHECK   VISA   MC   AMEX

(circle one)

Card # _____

expires _____ /_____

Please allow 4-6 weeks for delivery.